Alfred's Basic Piano Library

Chord Approach

A PIANO METHOD FOR THE LATER BEGINNER

Duet Book
LEVEL 2

D1490414

CONTENTS

FOREWORD

While this book of duets is correlated with the corresponding level of Alfred's Basic Chord Approach, teachers should be aware that the pieces are written in a manner which makes them highly adaptable to almost any other method. Later beginners will find the titles and the music fun and motivational. The secondo parts, which can be played by the teacher, parent, or a more advanced student, are delightful accompaniments which serve to enhance the student's part. The primo is "complete" in itself, thus creating little solos which become even more fun when performed as a duet! It is hoped that these duets will bring a smile to the faces of teachers, students, and audiences whether they are performed at the lesson, at home, or on the recital hall stage.

Dennis Alexander

DUET PART (Student plays 1 octave higher)

EASY DOES IT!

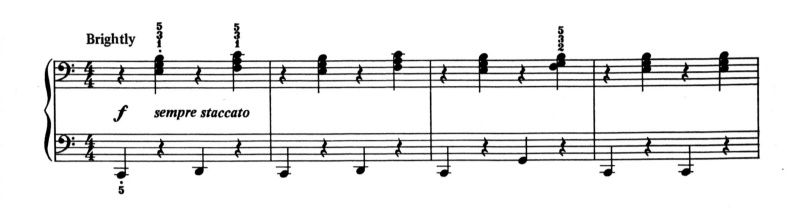

* The pairs of eighth notes may be played a bit unevenly, in a "lilting" style:

long short long short

Use after ON WITH THE SHOW, LESSON BOOK 2 (page 4).

EASY DOES IT!

* The pairs of eighth notes may be played a bit unevenly, in a "lilting" style:
long short long short

DUET PART (Student plays 1 octave higher)

CALYPSO RHUMBA

Use after ALOUETTE (page 10).

CALYPSO RHUMBA

8

WALKIN' COOL

Use after BLOW THE MAN DOWN! (page 14).

WALKIN' COOL

DUET PART (Student plays 1 octave higher)

"UPBEAT" WALTZ

Use after MEDLEY OF ENGLISH DANCES (page 15).

"UPBEAT" WALTZ

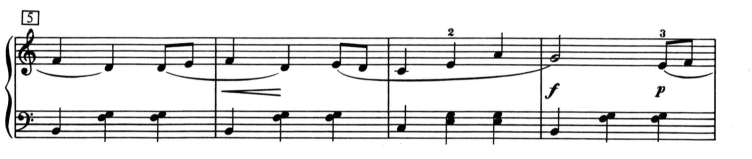

ritardando (2nd time only)

DUET PART (Student plays 1 octave higher)

ONLY YESTERDAY

Use after I'M GONNA SING! (page 17).

ONLY YESTERDAY

DUET PART (Student plays 1 octave higher)

MISSING YOU

Use after CAFÉ VIENNA (page 25).

MISSING YOU

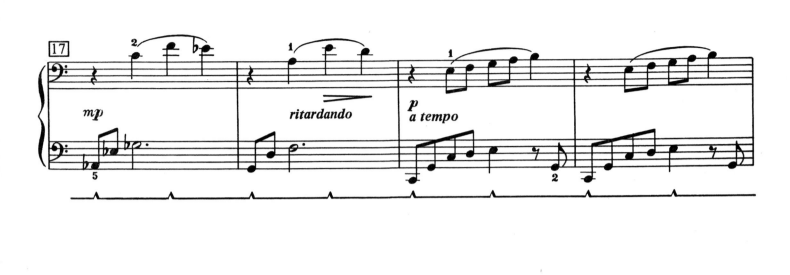

DUET PART (Student plays 1 octave higher)

MARCHING TRIADS

Use after COCKLES & MUSSELS (page 33).

MARCHING TRIADS

DUET PART (Student plays 1 octave higher)

GENTLE WINDS

Use after THE HARMONICA PLAYER (page 34).

GENTLE WINDS

DUET PART (Student plays 1 octave higher)

SONATINA IN C

Use after GOT THOSE BLUES! (page 37).

SONATINA IN C

DUET PART (Student plays 1 octave higher)

PINK ICICLES

Use after THE CANCAN (page 41).

PINK ICICLES

DUET PART (Student plays 1 octave higher)

UPTOWN WALTZ

Use after THE MARINES' HYMN (page 44).

UPTOWN WALTZ

DUET PART (Student plays 1 octave higher)

WHEN THE SAINTS GO ROCKIN' IN

Use after O SOLE MIO! (page 54).

WHEN THE SAINTS GO ROCKIN' IN

Moderately fast

DUET PART (Student plays 1 octave higher)

MOVIN' ON!

Use after STROLL IN THE PARK (page 58).

MOVIN' ON!

* The pairs of eighth notes may be played a bit unevenly, in a "lilting" style:

long short long short

** D.S. (Dal Segno) means "from the sign". D.S. 𝄋 al Fine means Repeat from the sign 𝄋 and play to the FINE.

Dennis Alexander

Since his affiliation with Alfred Publishing Company in 1986 as a composer and clinician, Dennis Alexander has earned an international reputation as one of the foremost composers of educational piano music for beginning and intermediate students. Currently a professor of piano at the University of Montana, Missoula, he teaches both piano performance and piano pedagogy, and coordinates the piano division. In 1987 he made his New York debut at Carnegie Recital Hall with violinist Walter Olivares and continues to be active as a soloist, accompanist and chamber musician.

Mr. Alexander is a past president of the Montana Music Teachers Association and has been a featured speaker at national conventions of the Music Teachers National Association (MTNA). In addition to writing all the duet books for Alfred's Basic Piano Library, he has recorded much of this successful method. His extensive output includes solo and duet repertoire in collections and sheet music for beginning through early advanced students.